BUNGALOW BASICS
PORCHES

By Paul Duchscherer

Photography by Douglas Keister

Pomegranate

SAN FRANCISCO

Published by Pomegranate Communications, Inc.
Box 808022, Petaluma, California 94975
800-227-1428; www.pomegranate.com

Pomegranate Europe Ltd.
Unit 1, Heathcote Business Centre, Hurlbutt Road
Warwick, Warwickshire CV34 6TD, U.K.
[+44] 0 1926 430111

Library of Congress Cataloging-in-Publication Data
Duchscherer, Paul.
    Bungalow basics. Porches / by Paul Duchscherer ; photography by Douglas Keister.
        p. cm.–(Pomegranate catalog ; no. A720)
    ISBN 0-7649-2891-0
    1. Bungalows–United States. 2. Porches–United States. 3. Arts and crafts
movement–United States. I. Title: Porches. II. Keister, Douglas. III. Title. IV. Series.

    NA7571.D824 2004
    728'.373–dc22

                                                                    2004044697

Pomegranate Catalog No. A720

Designed by Patrice Morris

Printed in Korea

13 12 11 10 09 08 07 06 05 04   10 9 8 7 6 5 4 3 2 1

This book is dedicated to the discovery,
appreciation, and preservation of bungalows,
and especially to all those who
love and care for them.

Acknowledgments

Because of space limitations, we regret that it is not possible to acknowledge each of those individuals and organizations who have helped us with this book. Our heartfelt appreciation is extended especially to all the homeowners who, by graciously sharing their homes with us, have made this book a reality. Special thanks are given also to Sandy Schweitzer, John Freed, and Don Merrill for their tireless support, unflagging encouragement, and invaluable assistance. We salute you!

At the end of the book, we have noted a few of the talented artisans, architects, designers, craftspeople, and manufacturers whose work appears here, but space constraints preclude us from crediting each one. We offer them all our deepest gratitude. Alternatively, our readers may wish to consult the extensive credit listings in our earlier book series, published by Penguin Putnam Inc. (comprising *The Bungalow: America's Arts & Crafts Home, Inside the Bungalow: America's Arts & Crafts Interior,* and *Outside the Bungalow: America's Arts & Crafts Garden*), which make reference to many of the images that are also included in this book.

W hen asked, "What is a bungalow?" most people will mention a front porch in their response. Even most dictionary definitions of *bungalow* list a porch (or veranda) as one of its defining features. The bungalow's intrinsic connection to porches originated in its distant Indian ancestor, the *bangala,* which had a high-pitched, thatched roof whose overhang shaded the structure's mud walls, creating a shallow veranda around the perimeter. In the United States, this concept was translated (albeit rather loosely) into the prominent, all-embracing rooflines that distinguish many Craftsman-style bungalows. Most of the illustrations presented here reflect the broad influence of the Craftsman style. Although this book's primary focus is on the front porch, examples of other inviting outdoor living spaces of bungalows are also included.

Long before 1900, when the bungalow phenomenon was in its early ascendancy, front porches were already a part of the American architectural vernacular. The front porches most familiar to Americans were the spacious ones (often decked out with wooden "gingerbread" trim) dating from the Victorian era, then at its close. Other variations had appeared on pre-nineteenth-century American homes, but these porches were far fewer in number and regionally limited. By the turn of the twentieth century, front porches had become a familiar streetside appendage on countless homes across the country. Row after row of porch-fronted houses lined the leafy residential streets of American towns and cities, and a drive through the countryside would suggest that every farmhouse had a front porch, too. Although the bungalow's reputation as the most modern house of its day accounted for much of its popularity, another likely factor was Americans' well-established fondness for front porches.

By reputation the bungalow came to be linked also to the concept of indoor-outdoor living. Then as now, the bungalow's smaller scale and low-slung form fostered a close relationship to its garden and the natural environment. The front porch served as a transitional space between inside and outside. Because many front doors opened directly into the living room, front porches became open-air anterooms, greatly increasing a bungalow's useable living space (at least seasonally, if not year-round) while allowing observation of the surrounding landscape. This association with the outdoors also stemmed from the bungalow's initial proliferation in areas with milder climates, particularly in California, where bungalows first won popularity as artistically designed yet affordable housing. Bungalows with front porches were a favorite subject of postcard imagery that flaunted California's verdant surroundings, tempting those from chillier climates to leave the snow behind and find domestic bliss in a rose-covered bungalow out west (Figure 6). Such bald-faced promotion proved to be an effective lure. Many people fell in love with bungalows simply from seeing them on a postcard. Visions of lounging on one's own shady front porch became a potent aspect of this American dream.

Fond of extolling the prospects of blissful family life in a bungalow, furniture manufacturer Gustav Stickley often hailed the healthful benefits of fresh air and outdoor living that bungalow porches could provide. In his magazine, *The Craftsman,* Stickley promoted his personal vision of a "Craftsman" way of life and published plans (which he also sold) of houses that he designed. He was not alone among enthusiastic bungalow proponents whose praise assigned near-mythic status to the advantages of bungalow living. Before long, many of Stickley's innovations—especially his beloved Craftsman style—were routinely copied by others. Similar ideas soon appeared in contemporary periodicals and design advice books that catered to the bungalow market (Figure 1).

Calling them "outdoor living rooms," Stickley believed that front porches should be fully furnished equivalents of the living rooms that adjoined them. Indeed, a minor obsession of period tastemakers like Stickley was how to properly furnish the porch. Some nineteenth-century favorites carried over into the bungalow era, in particular the porch swing, hammock, rocking chair, and furniture made of lightweight woven wicker or rattan (Figures 7, 21, 25–30, 35–37). A well-loved relative of the porch swing was the more earthbound glider. Another outdoor standby was the familiar Adirondack chair

(Figures 15, 28), many of which were built as weekend projects by handy husbands who subscribed to magazines such as *Popular Mechanics*. Some bungalow front porches incorporated built-in benches (Figure 31). Many more had railing walls with wide caps, which could double as bench-style seating (Figure 20). Textiles such as throw rugs, pillows, and blankets made porches feel like real living rooms. All these furnishings are still enlisted for use on many front porches.

The deep overhangs of porch roofs were often criticized for blocking too much light from interior rooms. One successful remedy was the use of a skeletal wooden framework to create an open-beamed pergola, usually attached to the house and extending over the porch area (Figures 4–5, 10, 13, 15–16, 23). While such airy structures didn't provide much shelter from the weather, their charming effect and the extra interior light they allowed made them a tempting alternative. In a variation, a solid roof covered part of the front porch; the remaining area was either covered by pergola-style beams or left completely open. Many of the bungalow plans published by Stickley featured architecturally integrated planters and pergola structures to support climbing vines (Figures 4–5), reflecting his interest in using vegetation to blend a house into its environment.

Today, the extravagant use of climbing vines on bungalow exteriors (Figures 6–7, 9) that Stickley and others once so strongly advocated is largely discouraged. Clinging ivy in particular can encroach on building materials such as masonry and cause real damage. Nonetheless, the effects of such vines (especially the flowering varieties) have undeniable charm. With diligence, some vining plants can be fairly easily kept under control (Figures 13–14). A safe way to add the look of vines to an exterior is to support them on separate trellises, kept several inches from the face of the wall by means of spacer supports. These trellises should have the ability to be pulled away from the house without damaging their "occupants," to allow for painting when the time comes (and it will). Trellises set against walls that don't require painting should be similarly positioned.

The Craftsman style's appeal steadily declined in the years after World War I, but that of the bungalow and the front porch did not; both continued to evolve. By the 1920s, the design influences that were replacing the once-predominant Craftsman style brought historicism back into the limelight. Sometimes called the "romantic revivals," they included the Colonial Revival, English Cottage, English Tudor Revival, and Spanish Colonial Revival styles. Most had their own signature elements, which were adapted to the front porch. For example, porches with a Colonial Revival influence had classical columns and other refined brick or millwork details (Figures 13, 35, 37, 48). Spanish Colonial Revival (and sometimes Mission Revival) bungalow porches frequently had stuccoed arcades (Figure 39) or a courtyard-like area behind a low wall (Figure 40). The English-influenced styles were typically expressed through particular forms of roofs, doors, and windows (Figure 3) or in Tudor-specific "half-timbered" exterior walls. Some English Cottage and English Tudor Revival bungalows did have conventional front porches, but this was due more likely to the enduring popularity of the front porch than to any historical reference. More often, the front porches of the English styles were reduced to much smaller-scaled (but still roofed) portico structures, which covered the front door but added no real living space (Figure 32).

Another shift in bungalow front porches, not specifically related to style, concerned the manner in which homeowners preferred to use them. Although open-air front porches were a staple of Craftsman bungalows, not everyone was convinced of their practicality. The enclosure of porches behind glass windows became a common occurrence across the country, especially in the harshest climates (Figures 42–43). Many bungalow owners decided to convert their front porch into an all-season room, greatly expanding its potential uses. However, since most porches weren't originally designed to be glassed in, the results were mixed. Often, a front porch enclosure compromised the home's street presence. While new owners of vintage bungalows may zealously "correct" other alterations to their home's original design, they may be reluctant to restore the openness of an enclosed front porch. Alas, a home's useable interior square footage still tends to be a higher priority than most aesthetic issues.

A bungalow likely made its major architectural statement through the particular form and detailing of its front porch. Craftsman-style porches often featured prominent masonry elements (of brick or stone) on the foundation facing (Figure 23), porch post piers (Figures 2, 28), low "railing" walls (Figure 3), or possibly on all three to lend a feeling of strength and permanence (Figures 1, 36). Tall, square (or trapezoidal) columns, most without piers, also might have been faced in stone, brick, or a combination of both (Figures 4, 7, 15, 19, 22). Important masonry details were likely repeated on the chimney (Figure 19). The use of two or more contrasting types of brick added variety of texture and color (Figure 34). "Clinker brick," with an irregular form, variegated color, and craggy texture, was especially popular in Craftsman applications (Figures 2, 8). Sometimes clinker brick appeared in eye-catching combinations with various kinds of stone (Figures 15, 20), a favorite masonry detail of the renowned period architects Charles and Henry Greene (Figure 16). The wide concrete caps that often topped low masonry walls provided extra seating and made useful ledges for decorative urns or flower boxes; occasionally they incorporated built-in planters (Figure 18).

A front porch's wooden elements also could be quite distinctive, sometimes more so than any accompanying masonry. Among the most common Craftsman-style features were columns of trapezoidal form, produced in widely varying proportions. Most perched atop bases of brick or stone, which also varied greatly in height and girth (Figures 2, 23, 34). While not all wooden porch posts tapered, most did have a square profile (Figures 3, 20, 27–28). To increase their visual impact, porch posts were sometimes closely placed in groupings of two or three (Figures 1, 14, 17, 33, 36). Interesting but less common were porch posts made of weighty tree trunks, often with their bark intact (Figure 24). Typical of the so-called Adirondack (or Rustic) style, such porch posts were used primarily on vacation homes or lodges. Some of these porches incorporated matching furnishings crafted from irregular tree branches. Americans' interest in this picturesque look dated back to the mid-nineteenth century, long before any Arts and Crafts influence, but because of their shared emphasis on handicraft and natural materials, the two styles were quite compatible. Classically detailed columns (both round and square) show the influence of the Colonial Revival style on bungalow porches, especially in examples from the 1920s. Simplified or abstracted versions of classical columns were popular supports for pergolas (Figures 3, 5, 12–13).

Capped by sturdy handrails, wooden railings often were used between columns or post piers (Figure 7). Craftsman-style railings commonly had plain, square balusters of a fairly weighty scale—at least two to three inches square, set with gaps of about the same dimension. Some open wood railings had slightly more complex patterns (Figures 9, 30) or unusual geometric designs (Figure 38). More substantial-looking railings could be created by using flat boards (about six to eight inches wide) for balusters, with proportionally smaller gaps between them (Figure 35). A variation on this railing style, inspired by those on Swiss chalets, featured decorative cut-out shapes on each board. Solid, low railing walls, described previously of masonry, were also often built of wood. Typically finished to match the adjacent wood siding or shingle-covered walls (Figures 10, 14, 47), they gave extra privacy to the porch's seated occupants. Probably the simplest kind of wood railing consisted solely of a handrail, either square or rectangular in profile (Figures 2, 27–28). Front porches constructed low enough to the ground might have had no railings at all (Figures 12–13, 31, 45).

A number of different treatments were originally used for bungalow porch floors. If the house and front porch were constructed entirely of wood, then the porch floor might have been surfaced with tightly fitted strips of softwood, usually painted with a durable enamel. Among the most common, least expensive, and most resilient floors were those surfaced in concrete, often scored with grid lines to mimic tiling. While some vintage concrete floors have remained in their original state, many have been painted later (Figure 39). If unpainted, concrete can be stained to achieve a warmer look today (Figure 36). Brick accents were used as borders or on steps (Figure 32). Entirely bricked or flagstone-faced floors were less common, although they were sometimes added later over existing concrete. Square terra-cotta tiles produced a more refined effect (Figure 29); when bordered in brick, they were a favorite choice for outdoor flooring of Greene and Greene, whose projects typically had very generous budgets (Figures 16–17).

The ceilings of many Craftsman-style porches were surfaced in narrow, interlocking boards, generally called beadboard or tongue-in-groove paneling (Figures 19, 35, 43). Sometimes the structural framing beams were left exposed (Figures 17, 26–28, 30). If the house was faced in stucco, then the porch ceiling often was finished to match (Figure 38), but not always. When properly sealed and finished, these durable surfaces could endure the rigors of an outdoor (albeit covered) location for many years and are among the least likely features to have been changed on most bungalows.

Lighting on bungalow porches varied widely according to budget, but most commonly it was provided by fairly inexpensive, utilitarian fixtures that didn't make much of a style statement (Figure 3). However, a considerable number of surviving original fixtures on Craftsman homes clearly were selected to coordinate with the archi-tecture (Figures 26–28, 30). This coordination reached its apogee on some of the grander examples of the style, such as the houses designed by Greene and Greene (Figures 16–17). Sometimes porch fixtures were mounted on the ceiling (Figures 29–30, 32, 36, 38), but more often they were wall mounted near the front door (Figures 3, 7–8, 23, 26, 33). Pairs of lights occasionally flanked the door (Figure 31). Larger porches could accommodate more than one ceiling fixture (Figure 29) or a combination of both wall and ceiling fixtures (Figures 28, 44). The most popular Craftsman lighting designs were Japanese-inspired lanterns (usually boxy in shape), with small overhanging "roofs" and (perhaps) colored art-glass panels.

Today, several manufacturers offer good reproductions of Craftsman-style light fixtures and shades at different price levels. Some are close copies of period designs (Figures 18, 48) while others are more contemporary interpretations (Figures 7, 31, 40). Vintage lights remain another option for bungalow owners, who will find an abundance of antique lighting resources available. Try to avoid the temptation of selecting fixtures that may be too large or too ornate for the average bungalow. Instead, select one that might have been there originally. Modern recessed downlights should never be considered for use on a historic bungalow's porch. Such an incongruous feature would somehow diminish that heartwarming expression uttered in many a bungalow, "I'll leave the porch light on for you."

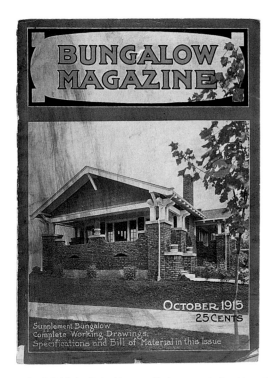

1. Well detailed with many Craftsman-style flourishes, the bungalow on the cover of the October 1915 issue of *Bungalow Magazine* has both a front and side porch, a bonus feature more typical of homes designed for corner lots. Published for several years by a prolific Seattle builder named Jud Yoho, this magazine was a convenient vehicle for promoting greater interest in his bungalows. A complete set of working drawings and specifications for the cover house came with the issue.

2. *(left)* An appealing trait that helped sell many homes, full-width front porches such as this one were a defining feature of Craftsman-style bungalows. While their form could vary considerably, most were determined by the roof's shape and gable placement. The front-facing gable that shelters this porch has typical "knee braces" projecting beneath its deep eaves. Short, tapering columns, as seen here, were also common. Less typical but still in the Craftsman mode, the railing is a single, stout square beam, which appears to penetrate the clinker brick piers.

3. This arched pergola, door, and low brick wall appear to be part of a small front porch, but are actually located on one side of a freestanding garage, which is in full view of a 1913 corner house. To upgrade this view, the visible side of the garage was made to resemble an English Cottage–style bungalow. In front of the brick wall, a low fountain is fed by water "spit" from a sea creature's face on a tile plaque.

BUNGALOW BASICS

❧ 4. An article about a new bungalow design in the April 1907 issue of Gustav Stickley's magazine, *The Craftsman*, promoted plantings as a way to ensure a home's harmonious blending with its setting. Instead of a typical front porch, a vine-covered, open-beamed pergola encloses a raised entry court. Flower boxes rest on stone walls; a larger window box accents a shed-roofed dormer above.

❧ 5. Another Gustav Stickley design demonstrating the use of plants to enhance a building, "Bungalow No. 124" was first published in a 1911 issue of *The Craftsman*. To reduce its cost, the house has minimal detailing, except for a full-width pergola-style front porch, which provides quite a visual boost. Open trellises, placed in front of low stuccoed walls, lighten their effect.

➣ 6. A 1918 postcard depicting "A Rose-Embowered Bungalow, California" flaunts that state's image as a year-round garden paradise. The popularity of postcards grew during the heyday of the bungalow, and somewhat idealized views like this helped promote the appeal of these homes nationwide. Vintage postcards provide glimpses of actual period landscapes. Supporting a thick canopy of flowering vines (which seem to envelop the entire bungalow), an open-beamed pergola shelters this front porch.

7. Nearly concealed by climbing foliage, which unites the house and surrounding garden, a pair of massive columns faced in river rock support the gabled roof overhang of this attractive front porch. Further linking the house with its site, river rock is used also as an edging for the densely planted front bed. A deeply cushioned swing, long a front porch favorite, invites relaxing. Lattice grids in the gables cover screened openings that allow for attic air circulation.

8. *(left)* Supporting one corner of a 1906 bungalow's porch, a tall column of clinker brick guides a slightly wayward blooming wisteria vine up and across the open beams of a pergola-style roof. Low brick walls enclose the porch, which retains its original front door, leaded glass sidelights, porch swing, and vintage lighting. The scene's lush profusion recalls old photographs of period bungalow gardens.

9. Framing two ladies admiring the garden, this vine-cloaked bungalow porch has most of its architectural detail obscured by a profusion of vegetation. Taken from Henry Saylor's popular 1911 design advice book titled *Bungalows,* this leafy image encouraged readers to take an aggressive planting approach; its caption insisted, "Do not fail to set out the rapid-growing vines as soon as the builders leave." Today, the prevailing opinion is that such clinging vines may be picturesque but can sometimes promote structural damage.

10. Also from Henry Saylor's *Bungalows* book, this image shows a porch that does not block light from adjacent interior rooms. Beneath a clipped (or jerkinhead) gable, the open-beamed structure of this side porch resembles that of a simple shed roof. Allowing more light to reach the windows, it also supports climbing vines. Instead of open railings, the porch area is enclosed by low shingled walls.

11. Cloaked in a mantle of wisteria in its full glory, the shadowy recesses of a 1905 shingled bungalow's front porch intensify the blooms' effect. Still a favorite of many today, wisteria was a popular choice for early-twentieth-century porches and gardens. After its flowers fade, the feathery green foliage provides extra privacy and shade during the warmest months, when front porches are most likely to be centers of outdoor living.

12. Oriented primarily toward a roomy side yard, this 1908 bungalow doesn't have much of a front porch, but it does have a three-sided courtyard created by its U-shaped floor plan, with two shallow wings of interior rooms overlooking a central fountain. A graceful pergola structure links the wings and widens into an outdoor dining area at right. Once entirely missing, the pergola was re-created by the current owners, who copied its design from old photographs provided by a previous owner.

✒ 13. Entwined with wisteria but not engulfed by it, the open wood
structure of this pergola-style porch rests on sturdy, simply detailed concrete columns. The open roof maximizes daylight admitted to the living
room (out of view, at left). The porch is part of the 1915 Lanterman House
in La Cañada-Flintridge, California, a rather large Craftsman-style bungalow
now open to the public as a house museum. The home's exterior has been
restored, while its original interiors and furnishings survive intact.

14. With two dormers (one with a balcony), a so-called cat-slide roof on the 1908 Charles Warren Brown house in Santa Monica, California, covers the front porch with an upturned sweep. The showy foliage of Easter lily vine *(Beaumontia grandiflora)*, kept in check by regular trimming, climbs up one corner and across the front eaves. To show off the house, most plantings around it are kept quite low.

15. *(overleaf)* Light passes through the vines and open beams of a pergola roof on the full-width front porch of a 1907 Craftsman-style home. The front door is located at the center of the house (out of view, at right), so only half of the porch is seen here. The columns and low walls have "peanut-brittle-style" masonry, which blends clinker brick with contrasting stones (similar to that seen in Figure 16). Adirondack chairs, with typically wide, flat arms and slatted, angled backs, sit on concrete flooring that is scored to resemble tiles (a preferred cool spot for the resident basset hound).

16. At Greene and Greene's 1906 Duncan-Irwin House in Pasadena, a large entry pergola shows off the architects' signature artistry with wood and masonry. With deliberately irregular textures and colors, the low walls and tapering columns are constructed of clinker brick, river rock, and boulders. During a recent restoration, much of the matted growth of old wisteria vines had to be removed. Original features include the pagoda-inspired copper lanterns and the home's street address carved into a granite boulder (out of view, at right).

17. Part of a covered front porch that adjoins a generous open terrace, this is one of several inviting outdoor living spaces at Greene and Greene's 1906 Duncan-Irwin House (seen also in Figure 16). Used as outdoor paving throughout are square terra-cotta tiles bordered with brick. The home's design, which artfully expresses a variety of natural materials, is actually the result of the Greenes' extensive remodeling of a smaller, previously existing bungalow.

 18. Covered by the deep eaves of a low gable on a circa-1910 Craftsman-style home, a private patio area is fully enclosed within the semi-circular sweep of a clinker brick wall. A narrow built-in planter projects from the wall's outer face, reducing the effect of its mass. Separated by a door that opens to a study, a pair of rounded bay windows (unusual for this style) repeat the wall's curving form. Lighting is provided by a copper-and-art-glass lantern suspended from a projecting beam.

19. Although entirely clad in river rock, these exterior walls and front porch columns are not of masonry construction; their structural framing is of wood. This pre-1900 bungalow shows vestiges of late-Victorian styling in its upper window sash divisions, arching stone details, and "eyebrow dormer" above the porch roof, yet its use of stone, visible rafter tails, and low-slung form betray an Arts and Crafts influence.

20. With a concrete cap and carefully placed accents of river rock, a clinker brick wall on a 1912 Craftsman-style bungalow rises from its foundation level to create the railing of this front porch. Integral to the wall's design is the tapering (or "battered") form of the brick pier. This view shows only one side of a spacious L-shaped porch, which can be accessed from both the dining room and front door of this corner house.

~ **21.** Set in a secluded redwood grove in Marin County, California, the 1904 summer home of anthropologist C. Hart Merriam has its front door and entry porch (at left) tucked under the sweeping roofline. Because the steeply sloping site prevented easy outside access from the main rooms that open onto this side of the house, the front porch's floor level was extended into a large raised deck area in the foreground (an original feature), providing extra living space.

~ **22.** *(overleaf)* Large, roughly shaped stones were stacked high to create the massive square columns of the front porch of an entirely stone-walled bungalow. Bedecked in its winter finery, the house is situated in the Cuyamaca Mountains east of San Diego, California. Such use of rugged natural materials recalls structures built by the government in the so-called National Park style (mostly in the 1920s and 1930s for motoring tourists).

23. *(right)* The main gable of this 1911 Craftsman-style bungalow runs perpendicular to the street, so the front porch is actually located next to the driveway, on one side of the house. The front door, flanked by narrow, full-height sidelights, retains its original wooden screen door. The epitome of Craftsman style, sturdy tapering columns support the heavy timber framing of a pergola-style porch roof, while river rock, shingles, and board-and-batten siding delineate different wall levels.

24. Built in the early 1900s, this shingled bungalow's front porch has some unusual columns, each made of a closely set cluster of four unpeeled redwood logs. Most often seen on vacation homes in mountain settings, the use of wood in its literally natural state was a hallmark of the so-called Adirondack style, which was also applied to furniture. Also called the Rustic style, this picturesque aesthetic actually predates the Arts and Crafts movement, but both approaches blend well together.

Living Room in a Live Oak.

25. This "Living Room in a Live Oak," pictured on a 1908 postcard, might resemble a fanciful tree house, but it more likely depicts the deck of a hillside house, built around some tree trunks. The unspecified location was likely in California, often the subject of postcards flaunting the lure of year-round outdoor living. The Native American rugs and simple furnishings would have been considered appropriate choices for turning a bungalow's porch into an "outdoor living room," as recommended by Gustav Stickley and other tastemakers of the era.

26. Creating an easy transition from outdoors to indoors, this 1911 bungalow's front porch has been cozily furnished as an outdoor living room. Bamboo blinds and an art-glass panel offer privacy and shade. A geometric-patterned rug lies underfoot; pillows soften a vintage wicker porch swing and chair. Fitted with beveled glass panels, the wide front door is a Craftsman classic.

➝ 27. If space permitted, some bungalows were designed with more than one porch. Although the front porch of this modest 1913 house is nice, it feels exposed to the street. However, halfway down the side driveway is this narrow, but far more private, porch area. Accessible from both the dining room (through French doors at right) and a small breakfast room (at the far end), it makes a convenient place to snack outdoors—and a quiet spot for Magic, the resident feline, to take a catnap.

28. From this comfortable vantage point, one can enjoy the civility of reclining in a porch swing or an Adirondack chair while savoring the wonders of nature so close at hand. Original features of this 1910s bungalow porch include the concrete floor (scored to resemble large tiles) and set of small lanterns hung from the beams. Outlooks are kept as open as possible by a single wood rail stretching between low river rock piers, which support square posts (the one in the center was added later).

29. A covered outdoor living space that is recessed into a home's exterior wall yet entirely open on one side (like this) may be called a loggia, a term first applied to similarly configured spaces in houses of much earlier periods. Quintessential "outdoor rooms," loggias are convenient, well shaded from hot sun, and sheltered from wind by their three-sided enclosure. More spacious than most at the time, this 1910 example opens to the interior through French doors. Shallow steps descend gently into a sunny rear garden.

⮞ 30. The 1907 Evans House in Marin County, California, sits on a steep hillside, and its primary rooms—including this covered rear porch— look across treetops behind it. Spanning the full width of the house, the porch has access to both the living and dining rooms through French doors (out of view). The wooden trough built into the railing once held planter boxes along the porch's entire length. The multipaned windows are removable. Original furnishings include the slatted oak swing and small lantern.

☙ 31. *(left)* Even if space is cramped, the front door still needs minimal shelter from the elements. A driveway passing close to the front of this modest 1910 bungalow left few porch options. The roof's overhang was extended to make an effective awning; tile flooring helps further define the area. New lanterns and bright red paint on the door, built-in benches, and window sash make the space feel more welcoming. The original garage survives at right.

☙ 32. This diminutive 1922 English Cottage–style bungalow has a charming street presence. Its clipped (or jerkinhead) gable ends are typical of that style, but the towerlike form of the small covered entry porch is unusual. While the porch doesn't add much outdoor living space, its peaked roof and decorative lattice panels offer extra visual appeal. Craftsman-style influence persists in the detailing of the exposed rafter tails.

33. On the front porch of a 1910s Craftsman-style home, a pair of French doors serves as the front door. To create balance and a better flow from interior rooms, an identical pair of French doors opens onto the porch at left. Groups of posts with stepped corbels resemble those in Figure 36. A low river rock wall and a color palette of deep greens and rust help blend the large house into its setting. This front porch offers a bonus: more outdoor living space on its roof.

34. Side-facing gables allow this 1911 bungalow's roof to sweep down low over its front porch. When seen from the street, it appears more modestly scaled. Other details common to the Craftsman style are the short, tapering porch columns, shed dormer, and exposed rafter tails (with decoratively cut ends) extending from the eaves. The various textures and colors of the bricks, siding, and shingles add further interest.

35. This view from a 1912 bungalow's front porch demonstrates the proximity to street and sidewalk typical of most bungalows. Although missing from many later housing designs, such useable front porches are appreciated today for encouraging neighborhood observation (which promotes security) and interaction with passersby. Such porch swings, very popular in the period, remain a favorite today.

36. Furnished as a truly luxurious outdoor living room, the front porch of the 1911 Henry Weaver House in Santa Monica, California, has rattan lounge furniture and a scattering of colorful, geometric-patterned textiles, including a Native American rug. The wooden ceiling is left unpainted, and the scored concrete floor is warmly tinted. Low walls of buff-colored brick rise at the corners into piers that support large square posts with stepped corbels. The tenons passing through the posts are more typical of Craftsman furniture.

37. Each of the gracefully arched openings of this 1920s bungalow's front porch has a central concrete keystone. Similarly shaped elements appear to either side of the larger arch at right. This detailing reflects the influence of the Colonial Revival style, then growing in popularity. Reinforcing the traditional feel of this style are the red brick-faced walls, white-painted wood trim, curved wicker furniture, and vintage rocking chair.

38. Otherwise quite typical in its features, this 1913 stucco-covered bungalow has a front porch that offers extraordinary visual interest from the street. Part of a well-preserved tract of developer-built bungalows, this one stands out among other design variations. In a mixed bag of style influences, the porch piers resemble Egyptian pylons, the wood rail's fretwork has an Asian feeling, the squared columns and windows suggest the Craftsman style, while the arch and fat corbels seem almost Mission Revival.

39. The front porch of this 1920s stucco-faced bungalow has detailing suggestive of the Mission Revival style, inspired by California's early missions. To evoke adobe construction, the style employs thick arches that form shadowy arcades like this. Echoing the arches are the large, curving brackets above the columns. A curved dormer vent recalls the decorative parapets that typically rise above Mission Revival–style rooflines.

✒ 40. A later variant of the Mission Revival, the Spanish Colonial Revival was among the most popular styles in 1920s bungalow design. With a typical red tile roof and stucco walls, this Spanish Colonial Revival bungalow also has an inviting patio area in front. The courtyard plans of California's early haciendas were sometimes adapted as modestly scaled central patios for some bungalows of this style, but more often the feeling of a courtyard was merely evoked by a low-walled, gated enclosure like this.

41. Although not Spanish-derived in architectural style, this simple circa-1900 bungalow does have a courtyard-like patio adjoining its front porch. For privacy, it is fully fenced off from the street. The roomy, brick-paved area expands this home's outdoor living space far beyond the limits of its narrow porch. An old wisteria outlines the eaves, but most of the plants are set in containers, allowing for flexible rearrangement.

42. As seen in this cozy example from the 1910s, many bungalow front porches were converted into inviting year-round living spaces by being enclosed in glass, especially in areas with harsher climates. The brick walls of this porch suggest that it was indeed open at one time, but the detailing of the arched windows indicate that it was enclosed relatively soon after the house was built.

43. A glass-enclosed porch on a 1910 shingled home in Plymouth, Massachusetts, has the same weather-resistant finishes that it sported during its days as an open-air space. These include an enamel-painted wood floor, shingled walls, and a wood ceiling of beadboard paneling. In the 1920s, the arched openings were filled in with casement windows and narrow glass transoms. French doors open onto a deck with woodsy views.

～ 44. Originally used as a sleeping porch, this spacious, sunny, window-lined room is now an informal living space, outfitted with a vintage set of rustic furniture made by Old Hickory. The walls and ceiling retain their board-and-batten paneling. A new maple floor has replaced the original flooring of asphalt roofing material. Designed by Pasadena architect Alfred Heineman, the 1909 Craftsman-style Gray House is located in the West Adams Historic District of Los Angeles.

~~ 45 & 46. A new Craftsman-style guest house on the grounds of the
1904 C. Hart Merriam House in Marin County, California (see Figure 21),
features an unusual concealed amenity that makes the most of a limited space.
The top photograph shows its small, covered front porch, which has a floor of
wooden decking. In the bottom photograph, a hinged panel discreetly built into
the decking has been raised to reveal a bubbling, recessed hot tub, ready for
use. The porch can thus switch functions at a moment's notice, from a shaded
outdoor sitting area to a soothing spa facility, both enjoying the same outlook.

BUNGALOW BASICS

❧ 47. A storage problem resulted in this ingenious front porch solution, part of a recent remodeling that changed this home's exterior style from 1920s Colonial Revival to a blending of the Craftsman and Shingle styles. The front of the new porch is outlined above by a gently curving arch (partly seen at upper right) and flanked by a pair of thick, tapering columns. This column's "secret" door opens to shelving for various small tools and garden supplies, while the other hollow column stores long-handled tools.

❧ 48. *(right)* This house lacked convenient access to its backyard from a bedroom that overlooked it. The problem was solved by the addition of a raised concrete terrace along the exterior wall, covered by an attached pergola that replicates original details from the front porch. A fine-mesh nylon screen, stretched across the pergola's top, gently filters sunlight. A new pair of French doors with matching sidelights allow easy outside access and admit more light inside.

BUNGALOW BACKGROUND

America's most popular house of the early twentieth century, the bungalow, is making a big comeback as our newest "historic" house. Surviving bungalows are now considered treasures by historic preservationists, while homeowners rediscover the bungalow's appeal as a modest, practical home with a convenient floor plan. This book highlights an important aspect of bungalow design.

Webster's New Collegiate Dictionary describes a bungalow as "a dwelling of a type first developed in India, usually one story, with low sweeping lines and a wide verandah." The word *bungalow* derives from the Hindi *bangala,* both an old Hindu kingdom in the Bengal region of India and a rural Bengali hut with a high thatched-roof overhang creating a covered porch (or verandah) around the perimeter to provide shade from the scorching sun. The height and steep pitch of the roof encouraged the hottest air to rise and escape, while cooler air flowed in at ground level (especially after sundown). The British colonists adapted the design in their own dwellings, and their success spread the concept from India to elsewhere in the British Empire, especially Southeast Asia, Africa, New Zealand, and Australia. By the late eighteenth century, the name *bangala* had been anglicized to *bungalow.*

This name first appeared in print in the United States in 1880.

Used in an architectural journal, it described a single-story, shingled Cape Cod summerhouse ringed by covered porches. By the 1900s, *bungalow* had become part of our popular vocabulary, at first associated with vacation homes, both seaside and mountain. The bungalow's informality, a refreshing contrast to stuffy Victorian houses, helped fuel its popularity as a year-round home. It had its greatest fame as a modest middle-class house from 1900 to 1930.

Widely promoted, the bungalow was touted for its modernity, practicality, affordability, convenience, and often-artistic design. Expanding industry and a favorable economy across the country created an urgent need for new, affordable, middle-class housing, which the bungalow was just in time to meet.

In America, a bungalow implied a basic plan, rather than a specific style, of modest house. Typically, it consisted of 1,200 to 1,500 square feet, with living room, dining room, kitchen, two bedrooms, and bathroom all on one level. Some bungalows had roomy attic quarters, but most attics were bare or intended to be developed as the family's needs grew. A bungalow set in a garden fulfilled many Americans' dream of a home of their own.

Widely publicized California bungalows in the early 1900s spawned frenzied construction in booming urban areas across the country. In design, most bungalows built prior to World War I adopted the so-called Craftsman style, sometimes combined with influences from the Orient, the Swiss chalet, or the Prairie style. After the war, public taste shifted toward historic housing styles, and bungalows adapted Colonial Revival, English cottage, Tudor, Mission, and Spanish Colonial Revival features.

Today Craftsman is the style most associated with bungalows. Characterized inside and out by use of simple horizontal lines, Craftsman style relies on the artistry of exposed wood joinery (often visible on front porch detailing). Natural or rustic materials (wood siding, shingles, stone, and clinker brick) are favored. Interiors may be enriched with beamed ceilings, high wainscot paneling, art glass, and hammered copper or metalwork lighting accents.

The word *Craftsman* was coined by prominent furniture manufacturer and tastemaker Gustav Stickley, who used it to label his line of sturdy, slat-backed furniture (also widely known as Mission style), which was influenced by the English Arts and Crafts movement. That movement developed in the mid-nineteenth century as a reaction against the Industrial Revolution. Early leaders such as John Ruskin and William Morris turned to the medieval past for inspiration as they sought to preserve craft skills disappearing in the wake of factory mechanization.

In both the decorative arts (furniture, wallpaper, textiles, glass, metalwork, and ceramics) and architecture, the Arts and Crafts movement advocated use of the finest natural materials to make practical and beautiful designs, executed with skillful handcraftsmanship. One goal was to improve the poor-quality, mass-produced home furnishings available to the rising middle class. Morris and a group of like-minded friends founded a business to produce well-designed, handcrafted goods for domestic interiors. Although the company aspired to make its goods affordable to all, it faced the inevitable conflict between quality and cost. However, its Arts and Crafts example inspired many others in England (and eventually in America) to relearn treasured old craft traditions and continue them for posterity.

As it grew, the movement also became involved in politics, pressing for social reforms. Factory workers trapped in dull, repetitive jobs (with little hope for anything better) were among their chief concerns; they saw the workers' fate as a waste of human potential and talent.

The idealistic and visionary English movement's artistic goals of design reform were more successful than its forays into social reform. Perhaps its greatest success, in both England and the United States, was in giving the public a renewed sense of the value of quality materials, fine craftsmanship, and good design in times of rapid world change.

The Arts and Crafts movement had multiple influences on the American bungalow. The movement arrived here from England in the early 1900s, just as the bungalow was becoming popular. Among its most successful promoters was Elbert Hubbard, founder of the Roycroft Community, a group of artisans producing handmade books and decorative arts inspired by Morris. Hubbard also published two periodicals and sold goods by mail order.

Gustav Stickley was another American inspired by England's important reform movement and soon was expressing this inspiration in the sometimes austere but well-made designs of his Craftsman style. Becoming an influential promoter of the bungalow as an ideal "Craftsman home," he marketed furniture, lighting, metalwork, and textiles styled appropriately for it. His magazine, *The Craftsman,* was a popular vehicle for his ideas and products, and he sold plans for the Craftsman houses he published in his magazine. The wide popularity of his Craftsman style spread the aesthetic sensibilities of the Arts and Crafts movement into countless American middle-class households, making it a growing influence on architecture and decorative arts here. (England in the early twentieth century remarkably had no middle-class housing form comparable to the American bungalow, but Australia has bungalows of that period, inspired by ours, rather than any from Britain.)

Other manufacturers eventually contributed to Stickley's downfall by blatantly copying his ideas and products and eroding his market share. Once Stickley's exclusive brand name, the word *Craftsman* was assimilated into general use and became public property after his bankruptcy in 1916.

Americans choosing the Craftsman style for their homes, interiors, and furnishings rarely were committed to the artistic and philosophical reforms of the Arts and Crafts movement; most were simply following a vogue. Prospective homeowners (and real estate developers) usually selected their bungalow designs from inexpensive sets of plans marketed in catalogs called plan books; few used an architect's services. Some people even bought prefabricated "ready-cut" or "kit" houses. First sold in 1909 by Sears, Roebuck and Company, prefabricated houses soon were widely copied. In the heat of bungalow mania, Sears and others offered tempting incentives to prospective bungalow buyers, such as bonus financing for their lots. For a time, it was said that if you had a job, you could afford a bungalow. But when jobs were in short supply as the Great Depression hit, many defaulted on their little dream homes, leaving their creditors stung.

The depression ended the heyday of the bungalow, but its practical innovations reappeared in later houses, then more likely to be called cottages. The post-World War II ranch house could be considered the legacy of the bungalow. Only recently has a rising demand for lower-cost houses triggered a reevaluation of vintage bungalow stock as viable housing. In response to public demand, the home planning and construction industries have reprised some of the obvious charms of the bungalow in new homes. A real boon for homeowners seeking to restore or renovate a vintage bungalow (or perhaps build a new one) is today's flourishing Arts and Crafts revival, fueled by the demand for a wide array of newly crafted home furnishings that reflect the traditions and spirit of the Arts and Crafts movement. ✒

CREDITS

Figure 13: Restoration by John Benriter. **Figure 14 (and cover)**: Landscape designer: Jim Matsuo. **Figure 33**: Painting contractor (and color consultant): Elder Vides, Painting Concepts. **Figure 35**: Vintage porch swing from Brent and Linda Willis, the Handwerk Shop; urn from Wildwood Garden Furnishings (design by Gertrude Jeckyll). **Figure 43**: Folding screen, side chair, and pedestal by David Berman, Trustforth Studios. **Figures 45–46**: Design and labor by Julie Haas, Bill Pringle, and George Gonzales. **Figure 47**: Architect and builder: John Tankard. **Figure 48**: Architect: Daniel C. Lawrence; construction: Elder Vides.

ARCHIVAL IMAGES

Figure 1: Courtesy the collection of Erik Kramvik. **Figures 4–5**: Courtesy of Dover Publications, Inc. **Figure 6**: From the collection of Douglas Keister. **Figures 9–10**: From the collection of Paul Duchscherer. **Figure 25**: Courtesy the collection of Robert and Jackie Gustafson.